daddy cool

daddy cool

humorous and meaningful quotes on fatherhood

edited by tom burns

BARRON'S

about this book

Daddy Cool brings together an inspirational selection of powerful, life-affirming, and humorous phrases about fathers and fatherhood, and combines them with evocative and gently amusing animal photographs that bring out the full comedy and pathos of the human condition.

We all lead busy lives, and sometimes we forget to tell our dads how much we love them and how grateful we are for everything they do. These inspiring examples of wit and wisdom, written by real people based on their true-life experiences, sum up the essence of fatherhood, and why our fathers will always hold a special place in our hearts. As one of the entries so aptly puts it—a father is a banker provided by nature.

So give him a great big hug (then ask him for some money!)

about the editor

Tom Burns is a writer and editor who has written for a wide range of magazines and edited more than a hundred books over the past ten years on subjects as diverse as games and sports, cinema, history, and health and fitness. From the hundreds of contributions that were sent to him, he selected the ones that best sum up what being a dad is all about—giving support, encouragement, and most of all, love.

I'm just as lucky as I can be, for the world's coolest dad belongs to me.

He is just the easiest person
to talk to and nothing ever seems
to surprise him.

Any man can be a father. It takes someone special to be a dad.

To become a father is not hard. To be a father, however, is.

Only when I got a little older did I realize that I'd given my dad an additional full-time job.

It is easier for a father to have children than for children to have a real father.

You know when your dad is really there for you—it's not something you ever have to think about.

Blessed indeed is the man who hears many gentle voices call him father.

And he's blessed because it's down to him that those voices stay gentle.

Children really
brighten up a
household.

They never turn
the lights off!

It is a wise father who knows his own child.

I used to think it strange that he
always seemed to know what I
wanted even before asking—
now I just think how lucky I am.

A wise child maketh
a glad father.

One father is worth
more than
a hundred
schoolmasters.

Others can teach you what
you know. A good father teaches
you how to be.

Dad taught me
everything I know.
Unfortunately,
he didn't teach
me everything
he knows.

Fathers send their
sons to college
either because they
went to college,
or because
they didn't.

A dad is someone you look up to, no matter how tall you are.

When in doubt, ask dad.

Even when he doesn't know,
at least he can say so and
point you in the direction of
someone who does.

My father didn't tell me how to live; he lived, and let me watch him do it.

A father's good example is the best teacher.

Dad, you're cool,
because although
you are silly,
you always look
after me when
I need you.

I cannot think of any need in childhood as strong as the need for a father's protection.

He was the only one who could put the shadows away and scare off the wardrobe monster.

A man's children and his garden both reflect the amount of weeding done during the growing season.

Fathers represent another
way of looking at life—
the possibility of an
alternative dialogue.

It's easy for a father to hear
himself talking.

All he has to do is listen
to his children!

What a father says to his children is not heard by the world, but it will be heard for posterity.

Dads give guidance for life from your earliest days.

Dads—they say little, but give a lot.

A look, a simple look, can tell
me all I need to know.

The fundamental defect
of fathers is that they
want their children to
be a credit to them.

A dad is a man who expects his son to be as good a man as he meant to be.

By the time a man realizes that maybe his father was right, he usually has a son who thinks he's wrong.

As you get older, try to listen to your father more and judge less.

Why are men reluctant to become fathers?

They aren't through being children yet.

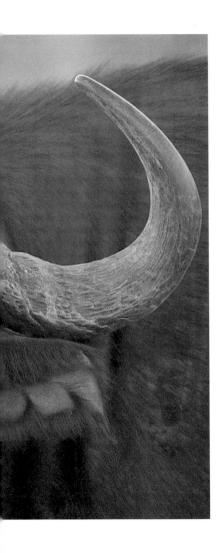

A truly great dad
never puts away
the simplicity of
being a child.

If he did, how could he assemble
train sets on Christmas morning
and play football in
the yard?

The child had
every toy
his father wanted.

There are three stages of a dad's life—he believes in Santa Claus, he doesn't believe in Santa Claus, he is Santa Claus.

Dad, you're sooooo
embarrassing…but
I love you.

Try to remember that, one day,
you'll be wearing clothes that
make your children cringe.

Having a family is like
having a bowling alley
installed in your head.

So just crack open a beer and
enjoy the game—it's not about to
end anytime soon.

Bottle feeding: an opportunity for dad to get up at 2 am too.

Fatherhood is pretending the present you love the most is soap-on-a-rope.

Q: What do you give the man who doesn't want anything?

A: Anything—he won't mind.

God can't fix everything…

…that's why he made
dads, and he made
them cool.

My dad can do anything—
fix it if it's broken, grease it if
it's squeaky, and build it if it
needs to be built.

Well, at least that's
what he thinks.

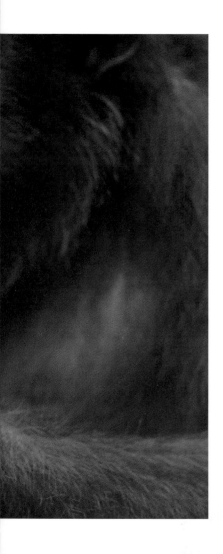

You know, dads just have a way of putting everything together.

Hell hath no fury
like a dad
whose tools are
messed up.

When your dad is
mad at you and asks,
"Do I look stupid?",
don't answer him.

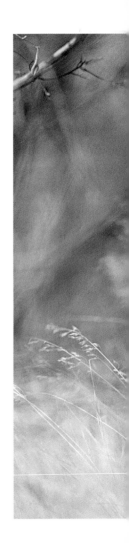

Love and fear.
Everything the father
of a family says must
inspire one or the other.

The most important thing
a father can do for his children
is to love their mother.

You don't have to deserve
your mother's love.

You have to deserve your
father's. He's more particular.

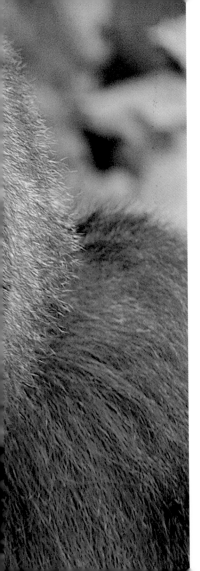

No child is
responsible
for his father.
That is entirely their
mother's affair.

Dad is the boss in the house;
mom is just the decision maker.

Try to think of yourself as a
shareholder—even if it's just
a minority one!

Mom says to dad:
It's your decision.

Mom means:
The correct decision
should be obvious.

If mom is the storm, then dad is the calm afterward.

In our house, the resolution to many an argument begins with the quietly spoken word, "Well…"

Dad is the keeper of keys, the lord of the airline tickets, and the king of the amusement park passes, theater tickets, and hotel confirmation numbers.

Everyone knows that dad is little more than chairman of the entertainment committee.

For which I say "Hooray! You can never have enough entertainment."

Mom says to dad:
You have to learn to
communicate.

Mom means:
Just agree with me.

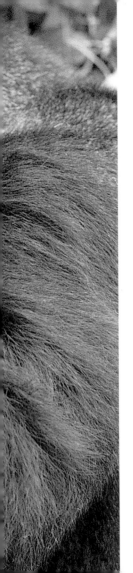

Mom says to dad:
Do you love me?

Mom means:
I'm going to ask for
something expensive.

Dad dreams, he plans, he struggles, so that we might have the best.

A father is a
banker
provided by
nature.

But be careful—no bank
is a bottomless pit.

You can always rely on dad cabs—twenty-four hour service, and no meter.

Never lend your
car to anyone
to whom you
are a dad.

That is the thankless position of the father in the family—the provider for a bunch of ingrates.

It is admirable for a man to take his son fishing, but there is a special place in heaven for the cool dad who takes his daughter shopping.

A cool dad is a guy who has snapshots in his wallet where his money used to be.

And they're probably snapshots of you, so bear it in mind the next time you ask for a loan.

A truly rich man
is one whose
children run into
his arms when his
hands are empty.

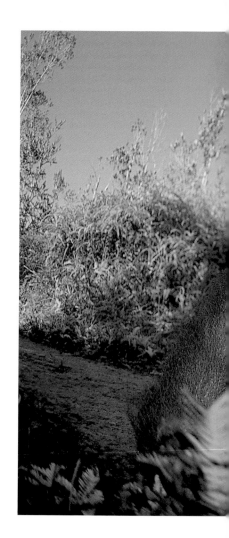

Sometimes the poorest man leaves his children the richest inheritance.

It's called love, so remember to pass it on.

My dad gave me
the greatest gift
anyone could give
another person—
he believed in me.

The greatest gift I ever had…
he is really cool… I call him Dad.